DON'T LET YOUR PAIN BE YOUR PRISON

God Can't Heal What You Don't Reveal

By Tajuana Brown

Stop Licking Your Wounds!
Be Consumed with What God Thinks About You!

Don't Let Your Pain Be Your Prison

For permission requests, contact: Purpose Publishing via email at contactus@purposepublishing.com.

For speaking engagements, interviews, bulk orders, or promotions, contact the author and stay connected at tajuanabrown777@gmail.com

Paperback ISBN: 978-1-965319-91-8
eBook ISBN: 978-1-965319-92-5

Editing by Mary Barvella Edits
Cover Design by Purpose Publishing

Printed in the United States of America

Purpose Publishing LLC.
13194 US Highway 301 South, Suite 417
Riverview, Florida 33578

www.PurposePublishing.com

TABLE OF CONTENTS

Chapter 1

THE BEGINNING OF SORROWS

My earliest memory of seeing brutality or abuse was seeing my mom lying on the kitchen floor while my dad was kicking her in her stomach. She tried to shield herself as well as she could while screaming his name, crying, and begging him to stop. I felt helpless. I was not afraid that he would hurt me next. I just wanted to help my mom, but I knew that I couldn't. She was pregnant with my little sister. Thankfully, they both survived the beating.

Later that night, we stood outside waiting for a cab. I looked up at her and saw blood streaming down her face. I was crying because she was crying. I was happy she seemed okay and glad that we were leaving.

We stayed with one of my mom's relatives for a while, but we would soon return home. I was four years old at that time. I attended daycare at a lady's house down the street. I rode my purple tricycle up and down my street and parked it in front of the house I was visiting. I loved that tricycle! That's how my mom knew how to find me.

My dad wasn't always like this. He was diagnosed as manic depressive. Today, it would be called bipolar disorder. He was prescribed a medication called Lithium. However, it didn't stop him from becoming a completely different person every two years in the spring.

When he was well, he was talkative, intelligent, and a very sharp dresser. He was an architect who designed beautiful buildings. He also drew and created abstract paintings. But you could set your calendar and know when changes were coming.

He would start to get very quiet. He would stay home more, his style of dress would be more subdued, and he would start wearing these strange oils and boil ginger root. I don't know what he did with the ginger, but the smell was nauseating. When we noticed these changes, Mom would hide the weapons in the house. He had a decorative samurai sword and a gun. The final stage brought violence.

It didn't take much to trigger him. The four of us would sit at the table for dinner. My seat was across from his. I would look up from my plate and see him just glaring at me. The next thing I knew, a plate of food would fly by and hit the wall behind me. Sometimes he would hallucinate. During dinner one night, he accused me of throwing potato salad at him. Of course, I had done no such thing. I hadn't thrown anything or even thought about doing it. All I could do was apologize and hope he would calm down.

I imagined him just flipping the whole table on me. Needless to say, I was very jumpy. If anyone raised their voice at me, my bladder would just give way, and I would be standing in a puddle. It was so embarrassing!

As I walked home after school every day, the closer I got to my house, the more slowly I would walk. I never knew what situation I would be walking into. I was so fearful. I was sorry for my mom. My dad didn't allow her to work. At least I was able to get away for a few hours when I was at school . H owever, she was stuck at home all the time.

When my dad was sick, we had to keep a bag packed. We never knew when we would have to run. If he became too violent with my mom, it wasn't safe to stay in the house with him. He would disable the car, so we had to jump fences and hide behind bushes to get away and catch a bus. Our options for places to go were limited because Mom didn't have any family in our town. Since she didn't go out of the house much, she didn't have any friends who weren't also Dad's friends. He would usually find us, though we did manage to get a few days of peace before we had to return home. I often wondered why my mom kept going back. It was years later before I finally figured it out.

His sickness would last for two to three months. Then he would return to his normal self. Sometimes we had to have him committed to a mental institution, but he could get out of a strait jacket in less than ten minutes! One time, he escaped from the hospital. My mom and I were so afraid. We knew he was going to come back home. He didn't have a car, so my mom thought of the easiest route he would take. We found him walking down the street in his blue robe. He was so happy to see us, but my mom immediately took him back to the hospital.

My escape was school. There I could be normal. I could pretend that everything was perfect and forget about what was going on at home. From kindergarten to the 12th grade, I only had one C. The rest of my grades were A's and B's, and I was often selected to be the emcee for elementary school assemblies.

I would sometimes laugh to myself because my teachers had no clue what was going on in my life.I was selected to participate in programs for gifted students. Once a week, I went to a different school to study music. By the time I graduated from sixth grade, I had learned how to play seven different instruments: the ukulele, recorder, autoharp, marimba, hand bells, steel drums, and the melodica!

The melodica is a handheld free-reed instrument similar to a pump organ or harmonica. It features a musical keyboard on top. I was also introduced to the violin during this time. I took private lessons. When we moved back to my parents' hometown, I played the violin in my school orchestra. I still play every Sunday at my church.

The years that my dad didn't get sick, I ended up being hospitalized because of a heart condition that was detected when I was two years old. It amazed me that every year, one of us would end up in the hospital! I was diagnosed with supraventricular tachycardia.

There were times when I was riding my bike or playing with my friends that my heart would start beating rapidly, sometimes as fast as 200 beats per minute. A person could stand across the room from me and see my heart beating. My vision would blur, and I remember feeling weak. My parents rushed me to the hospital so they could stabilize me. Sometimes I ended up staying for a few days.

I remember going back to school wearing a heart monitor that looked like a transistor radio. I couldn't do many strenuous activities. I was able to opt out of some of the gym requirements at school. I always took it in stride.

When I was hospitalized in the 5th grade, I remember it being a longer stay than usual. I got bored, so I asked the nurses at the nursing station if they needed help with anything. I read to the children in the playroom. I also helped with some light filing. They paid me by showing me where all the ice cream, juice, and treats were stored! My mom also brought me snacks. It was so cool to just walk down the hall and grab some ice cream or drinks to go with what she'd brought for me.

Chapter 2

STRONG HOLD

I started reading the Bible in elementary school. We didn't go to church, but one of my mom's aunts gave her a Bible, and she let me use it. I started reading it out of fear. One night, my mom told me she had heard an old man's voice coming from the bedroom I shared with my little sister. I immediately asked her if the voice was coming from my sister or me. She said she couldn't tell because it was dark in our room. I had seen *The Exorcist* and did not want to be possessed.

My father didn't tell us at the time that an old man had died in the house before we moved in. The Bible was the answer. I didn't understand everything that I was reading, but I learned that God could do miracles.

I remember looking outside my window and up into the sky and praying for my dad not to get sick. His time was coming up. I was in the 6th grade. I also prayed that none of my siblings would inherit this illness. Spring was approaching, and I noticed the signs. He was beginning to get quiet, so I prayed even harder. My prayers were working! He snapped out of it and started acting normal.

This was also the year that he decided to move back to his hometown. We moved before the end of the school year.

I was upset that I couldn't finish the school year and be part of the end-of-year concert. I was to be featured playing the steel drums. I had to teach my part to someone else. My mom wasn't happy about it, either. Neither of us understood why we couldn't wait until summer officially started for me so that I wouldn't have to miss everything.

On the day of the move, I remember looking at my dad as he drove the car. The closer we got to our destination, the quieter he became. When we finally got there, I could tell immediately that he had retreated, that his depression was setting in. What happened to my prayers? Was his depression just delayed? This time, he never recovered as he had before.

I didn't understand it then. Later, I realized that his mind was in a mental fortress from which he couldn't break free. Oddly enough, after we moved, I didn't have to be hospitalized again because of my heart condition while I was still in school.

We moved into a house that had been in my father's family for many years. It was an old three-story house. It shared a courtyard with the house my grandparents lived in and a building that used to be the slave quarters in the back of the courtyard. My dad renovated that building and turned it into apartments that could be rented out. I was wary of moving into the main house. Stories were going around that any couple who lived there would be divorced within six months. In the wee hours of the morning, when everyone was in bed, I would hear the sound of someone walking around with heavy shoes. My grandfather said he had heard the same thing when he lived alone in that house decades earlier.

The couple who lived there before we did was my aunt and uncle. They didn't stay in the house long. In fact, after they left, they moved clear across the country! My dad, an amazing architect, remodeled the third floor of the house for our living space. He planned to open the first and second floors to the public because it was a historic site. He only completed the third floor before our family fell apart.

The third floor was beautiful! There were marble floors and chandeliers. It could have easily been featured in a magazine. Nevertheless, we were miserable. The beatings didn't stop for my mom. At one point, I thought that he had finally killed her. She just collapsed on the floor and stopped moving. I stood there frozen. Whenever they started fighting, my little sister begged me to call the police, but I was too afraid to call. I was too busy thinking about what he would do to punish me. No way was I going to get involved!

My last punishment was still fresh in my mind. One night, I didn't eat all my rice for dinner, so he gave me a plate of plain white rice with nothing on it. I tried to eat it, but I couldn't stomach it plain. I remember picking peas out of my chair that I had dropped during dinner to make it more bearable. I eventually started gagging and threw up the rice.

My dad then gave me a choice. I had to either eat the rice that was now mixed with vomit or get a spanking. I opted for the spanking. I figured after a few pops on my bottom, it would be over. I was so wrong.

He told me to go to my room, take off my clothes, and lie on my stomach. Then he proceeded to beat me with an extension cord. I squeezed my eyes so tightly that my mom thought I had two black eyes. She asked if he punched me! After he was done, I couldn't lie on my back without pain.

To this day, I still can't eat white rice unless I have meat or vegetables on it! Coincidentally, I had a doctor's appointment the next day. I was hoping they would take me away from him. Either they didn't see the scars on my back, or they ignored them.

Months later, during one of my dad's rages, my mom collapsed. He kicked her unconscious body, but she didn't move or cry out. My dad snapped out of his rage. He picked up her limp body and placed her on the bed. I was so upset with myself for being too afraid to help her. If she were really dead, I was going to kill him. I knew where Mom hid the gun. Finally, she started to move, and I was able to breathe again.

I started looking more like my mom as I got older. When I was twelve years old, my dad started hitting me like he hit my mom. When my mom had to explain my fat lip or black eye to people, she finally decided it was time to leave him and the situation. She wouldn't leave for herself, but she had to keep her daughters safe. We found a relative my dad didn't know about to stay with. My mom, my sister, and I shared a room with my little cousin. My mom had the bed. We girls slept in sleeping bags. We didn't have much, but we were happy. Most importantly, we finally had peace from the fear of being beaten.

Chapter 3
MOM'S STORY

My mom shielded us as much as she could from Dad. She would go to the front of the house when we went to bed. Dad would follow. His goal was to keep her at a distance so that she wouldn't try to take us away. Mom's goal was to let us get enough sleep for school the next day. She became a junior car mechanic. My dad would disable the car to prevent us from leaving when he was away, so Mom learned how to reconnect car batteries and spark plugs. We left him many times, but we always went back. I wondered why it had taken so long for her to leave him for good. Years later, I discovered the reason.

When Mom was only about nine months old, her mother left her and her three siblings. Her grandmother raised her on a farm. Her father drank a lot and wasn't around much. Her grandmother gave her all of the love that she could. Her oldest brother was a loner and didn't interact much with her and their other two siblings.

Mom had fun growing up on the farm. Sometimes she didn't like the fact that no one else was around, but she has fond memories of some of the farm animals. They had a red pig that was nice enough to let her ride on its back. The black pig was mean and would chase her away. She and her sister would ride the mule together on Sunday evenings. When she came home from school, her grandmother always had cornbread or biscuits and syrup waiting for them.

As she got a little older, my mom was passed back and forth between different aunts and uncles. Her dad would come and go. She was too young when her mother left to miss her. Mom stayed to herself and did as she was told. She didn't have any dreams about what she wanted to do when she grew up. She simply existed day to day. She was just there.

Mom met my dad when she was working as a secretary at a law firm. She was only nineteen years old. Dad was a city architect. He noticed her because she had to go to the post office every day for the law firm. He followed her back to where she worked and told her she was the prettiest lady he had ever seen. They started dating shortly thereafter. She didn't know that he was married with four children.

One thing led to another, and she became pregnant with me. Mom was living with her sister, who was very upset about the pregnancy and wanted her to give me up for adoption. Mom refused and was miserable staying there, so she followed my dad to Florida. He was there on a business trip.

At first, she stayed with one of my dad's friends, Evelyn. Her husband was a musician and wasn't around much, but when he came home to stay for a while, he didn't want Mom there anymore.

This is where I was born. It was also the first time that Mom experienced my dad's mental illness. He came to pick her up when I was a couple of days old. They stayed at a hotel. She thought he was just sick with a cold or the flu. She didn't realize what was going on. He would sleep all the time.

He left her in Florida and returned to their hometown. She didn't hear from him for several days, so she reached out to his mother. She told Mom that he was sick and in the hospital. What Mom didn't know was that he was in a mental hospital.

Mom was running out of money and wanted to return home as well. She asked one of my dad's business partners in Florida for money to help pay for the trip. He gave her two choices: she could sleep with him and fly home, or ride the bus if she refused. Mom was shocked and disgusted. She took the second option and rode the bus back to her hometown.

Mom stayed with a friend when she returned. Yet not long after, she got really sick. Her appendix almost ruptured, and she had to have an emergency appendectomy.

She was in the hospital for a week. During that time, one of her aunts came and picked me up from Mom's friend's house. I was only a few months old. After Mom was released from the hospital, she also stayed with her aunt for a while. My dad started coming to see her. They eventually got married and moved to an apartment in town. She stayed with him for as long as she did because he would beg her to come back and promise to do better. She loved him and worried about what would happen to him if she wasn't there.

Although it seemed like the bad overshadowed their relationship, they did have some good times in their marriage. My dad was instrumental in helping my mom find her mother after thirty years of not knowing who she was. Mom kept thinking about her and decided it was time to find her. She knew that she lived in New York. She didn't blame her for leaving, but she did blame her for never reaching out to the children she left behind. At first, my grandmother didn't want to be found.

One weekend, Mom and Dad went to New York to find her, but the number they'd been given was wrong, and the address was too. Their car broke down. Mom got discouraged and wanted to give up, but Dad pushed her to keep going.

They eventually found Mom's mother. She explained why she left. Like Mom, she, too, was in an abusive relationship. She knew that if she stayed, my grandfather would have killed her.

She left and took the children several times, but he would always find them and bring them home. She would return home only to be beaten up again. The last time she left, she did take my mom and her sister. My grandfather came and took them away from her again. Unlike before, Grandma ran without looking back. She had a nervous breakdown.

After some time had passed, she was able to create a new life. She learned to love again and had another daughter. I believe Mom and Grandma bonded over their shared experiences. They had a relationship for over thirty years until Grandma passed away a few years ago. The pattern was already set.

Even though Mom didn't grow up with a mother's love, she poured so much love into my sister and me. I believe she gave us what she wished she had. She supported our dreams and did her best to help us succeed in life. I watched her grow into the strong woman that she is now.

Like Grandma, she created a new life after she finally left my dad. For so many years, she wasn't allowed to work. She stepped up and did what was necessary to support my sister and me. She refused to live in government housing. We stayed with one of her half-sisters until she saved up enough money for our first apartment.

She would catch a bus at 5 a.m. and stay on a family member's porch until it was time to go to work. She has worked for the same company for over thirty-five years!

My mom worked her way up to become a store manager at the local U-Haul. At one point, a picture of her face was on the side of the vans. She stepped down from the manager position a few years ago. Forty hours is like part-time to her. She's in her seventies now and still works full-time and cuts her own grass!

I watched her learn to love again. She met her second husband, Bill, at work. It took her a while to warm up to him after he started calling her. Then he started writing her notes and letters and eventually asked her out. They bonded because both of them had bad first marriages.

Chapter 4
COLORBLIND

My dad wasn't exactly fond of white people. Prejudice can be seen on all sides at different times. I remember receiving a white Barbie doll during a Christmas gift exchange in elementary school. When I started playing with it at home, my dad tore it apart, limb from limb, threw each part of that Barbie doll across the room, and forbade me from ever bringing any "white" Barbie dolls into the house!

His message was received—loud and clear. I didn't interact with many people outside of my race because my schools at that time were predominantly Black. I didn't have any bad experiences except the one with my dad. The Caucasian teachers that I had were all friendly.

Years after my parents separated, Mom came home and told my sister and me that she had met someone she wanted us to meet. His name was Bill, and he was white. It didn't matter to me if he was "green"! I saw firsthand how much horror she went through with our dad. I just wanted her to be happy. My little sister agreed. I must admit that it was a little awkward at first. I noticed people looking at us when we all went out together.

They eventually married. When Bill lived with us, I began to notice that there weren't many differences between us. We would speak openly and ask questions. The biggest difference was that we couldn't wash our hair every day like he could. Some of his food choices were questionable. He liked canned pinto beans and brussels sprouts. On Thanksgiving, he was happy with just turkey breast and white gravy made from a packet. I'm sure he felt the same way about some of the things that we ate, like lima beans and smoked neck bones! At the end of the day, he was just a man who loved my mom dearly.

I never saw them argue. I never heard him raise his voice at her or hit her. He never tried to replace our dad or discipline us. He would, however, tell on us if we did anything bad. Mom was the disciplinarian in the house. It helped us see that men didn't have to be brutes.

When we had gatherings with extended family members, he fit right in. Everyone embraced him. Everyone wanted my mom to be happy. Bill was a good part of my life from the time I was fourteen to about thirty-five. The more time I spent around him, the less I knew him as a white man. He was just my stepdad, Bill.

When I went to college, he encouraged me to do well. He wrote letters to me that always included his popular quote, "Books, Not Boys!" I had a partial scholarship to help with my school costs. Every semester, Bill would pay for my books. He went with me to buy my first car. He helped me learn how to drive a stick-shift car. When I got married, he walked me down the aisle and gave me away. We both cried a little. He's the only grandfather that my son Daniel ever knew and spent quality time with. We were blessed to have him in our lives.

When I told people about him, I didn't even think to mention his race. I remember a few times that I got some really funny reactions. He and my mom came to visit me at work during one of their vacation visits. I introduced him as my stepdad around the office.

At the end of that day, my supervisor came to me smiling and said, "You could have told me!"

I was clueless about what he was talking about.

Then he said, "You could have told me that your stepdad was white!"

We all just started laughing. The same thing happened when I took my husband, Chris, to my hometown to meet my parents for the first time when we were dating. I told him all about Bill. However, it never crossed my mind to mention his race. Bill opened the door for us, hugged me, and shook Chris's hand. Later in the evening, when Chris and I were alone in the living room, he said the same thing that my supervisor did, "You could have told me that your stepdad was white!"

I resisted making a smart remark like "He is?"

Because of Bill, I became colorblind. I don't immediately judge anyone because of the color of their skin. I look at people the way God does: "for man looketh on the outward appearance, but the LORD looketh on the heart" (1 Samuel 16:7, KJV).

If you are a nice person, you are all right with me. The world would be a much better place if more people felt this way. People come in many different shapes, sizes, and colors. At the end of the day, we are all people. Just like roses come in many different shapes, sizes, and colors, at the end of the day, a rose is still just a rose. As my pastor would say, "If you want to color God anything, color him Love!"

Chapter 5

INNOCENCE LOST

In the midst of living with domestic violence and heart issues, I was also molested by two family members and during two babysitting experiences. Before we delve deeper into this chapter, I want to make it known that I did not speak out. I didn't let anyone know about what was happening to me.

The first time was when I was three or four years old. When I think back, I can feel the pattern of the quilt that was on the bed—small balls under my little fingertips. The room was dark. I was with one of my older male cousins. I remember feeling a burning sensation in my private parts. I didn't cry. I didn't understand what was happening. I wasn't afraid of being around him later. I guess I put the memory too far back in my subconscious.

Years later, when I was in elementary school, I experienced inappropriate touching from my babysitter's brother. I was left in a room alone with him. I didn't say anything. I just sat there. I guess I was trying to understand the sensations that I was feeling. He stopped when someone walked back into the room.

He even showed up at my school one day. I was one of the safety patrols. We would get out of class about fifteen minutes before school was over. My post was at one of the crosswalks. My job was to press the traffic light button so kids could cross the street safely on their way home. He stopped by my post and talked with me for a while. I can't remember what he said because I tried not to listen. Thankfully, by the time I was ready to leave, he was gone.

My third encounter was more intense. My parents were going out for the evening, and our usual babysitter wasn't available. My mom went to pick up the new sitter and bring her back to our house. Apparently, my mom got lost along the way. It took her a while to come back home. I wonder if it was a sign that she shouldn't trust this person. Once my parents left us, the night started off normal. I was at my usual spot in front of the television. My sister was a toddler and was put to bed earlier.

The babysitter asked me if I wanted to play house. I foolishly said "yes." I didn't realize what playing house would entail. It ended up being a full-on make-out session. I remember my body tingling and my lips burning. Thankfully, my mom didn't use her again.

My defense mechanism to handle these things was to quickly forget that they ever happened, but different things would trigger my memory. It would come back to me while I was watching a movie or covering certain topics in my health class. As quickly as the memory came back to me, I buried it again.

This trauma-related condition is called dissociative amnesia. The brain blocks out distressing or overwhelming memories. The memory is not gone. It can be triggered by sights, emotions, or situations that resemble the original trauma. It is a protective response when something is too overwhelming. My brain compartmentalized the memory to help me function and survive. This is why my parents didn't know what was happening to me.

Memories would resurface briefly, only to disappear again, because my brain would quickly say, "This is too much."

I don't know whether it was due to these experiences, but by the time I was fifteen, I became sexually active. My parents had separated permanently at this point.

I got pregnant and miscarried before I even realized what had happened. I noticed that my period was late. I asked my cousin, who had a baby the year before, for advice.

She asked if I was throwing up. My response was "no." I didn't really have any symptoms other than the late cycle. Since I was not throwing up, she told me that I wasn't pregnant. I didn't realize that women are different, and we don't all have the same experiences during pregnancy. I noticed that my stomach was getting a little bigger. I shrugged it off. My "expert" had already told me that I wasn't pregnant. I was working part-time at a fast-food restaurant.

During one of my shifts, I started bleeding very heavily. My stomach started cramping. The pain was so excruciating that it took my breath away. I couldn't walk. I could only crawl because the pain was so intense.

My mom came and took me home. The pain lasted for hours. At one point, I felt like I had to throw up and have a bowel movement at the same time. As I sat on the toilet, I felt like something was coming out. I pulled it out the rest of the way. It looked like a piece of liver. I immediately felt so much better.

My mom took me to my first OB/GYN appointment shortly after this event. Even though I was only fifteen, I was able to put myself on birth control pills without parental consent. I then began to jump from one relationship to the next with very little space in between. I became the cliché "Looking for love in all of the wrong places."

The summer before my senior year in high school, I visited my favorite aunt and uncle. I loved staying with them. They were always nice to me. My aunt would bake chocolate chip cookies. They had a big, beautiful house with lots of land. My uncle was taking a course and needed help with math, which was one of my favorite subjects.

As I sat down at the table to help him, he pulled out a chair for me. He put his hand on the small of my back, but then his hand slipped lower and grazed my backside. I shook it off. That had to have been an accident, right? As the day progressed, it seemed like he was looking at me differently, almost appraisingly. I told myself that I was just imagining this.

The next night, we were watching television. Later, my uncle and I were the only ones left in the den. He took my hand, placed it on his lap, and asked if I was experienced. I was about to ask, "Experienced in what?" when my aunt walked back into the room. He moved his leg so that my hand fell away from him. Well, there was no more mistaking what his intentions were. I did my best to avoid him from then on.

I could not believe this. I was so disillusioned. I don't know if it was a coincidence, but the lock on the room I was staying in was broken. I couldn't lock my door! Any footsteps in the hall made me sit and prepare to run and scream. I had to stay alert and awake until I heard my uncle snoring. As the days went by, his touching became bolder. I tried to stay out of his reach.

One night, I was watching television across the room from him. My aunt called for him, so he went toward the back of the house to find out what she wanted. When he returned to the living room, he grabbed my hand to stroke his genitals while telling me that their son wasn't feeling well. I moved my hand away in horror. I was so disgusted. For weeks after I returned home, I kept rubbing my hand to rid myself of the feeling of him. In no way had I invited that behavior.

The final straw was when he grabbed my breast. I quickly jumped up and ran to my aunt. I stood in front of her, but I couldn't utter a single word. Would he say I had invited or tempted him? Would my aunt believe him or leave him? I didn't want to be the cause of them getting a divorce. I remembered how hard it was for them to have their son. In that moment, I decided to give my cousin what I didn't have at the time—a mom and a dad living together under the same roof.

My uncle wasn't a violent man that I knew of. He was just a pervert. I vowed to leave and never return. With my silence, he and his family could have a happy life. I hope I made the right decision. I hope that his actions during that trip were a once-in- a-lifetime lapse in judgment on his part.

The experience with my uncle really hurt me. All the memories from earlier in my childhood came flooding back, and for the first time in my life, I couldn't forget. I threw myself into the activities of my senior year of high school. School once again became my safe place. I was a member of the Beta Club and was inducted into the National Honor Society. Outside of school, I was a violinist in my hometown's youth symphony. I also had my part-time job. I was too busy to dwell on anything. I received a partial scholarship for college when I graduated. Things were looking up for me. Then everything came crashing down again.

Before I left for college, I had to take a physical exam to ensure all my vaccinations were up to date. I also had to see my cardiologist to check my heart. During the exam at the heart clinic, they noticed something very concerning. We were basically told that my heart could just stop pumping at any minute. We got a second opinion and were told that it wasn't as serious as they initially thought. I was given the green light to proceed with my college plans of studying to become a computer programmer.

I still couldn't get that first diagnosis out of my head. All of my memories of abuse came rushing in again. I questioned my sexuality. I remembered the experience with the female babysitter. I did not push her away. Did this mean I was bisexual? It became too much. I just wanted everything to end.

My grades started to suffer. For the first time in my life, I was getting C's instead of A's and B's. I was in danger of losing my scholarship. I started to play Russian roulette with my life. I would cross the street without looking for oncoming traffic. If I made it to the other side safely, I was meant to live another day. I had a few close calls.

The turning point came one night when I was alone in my dorm room. I started watching a church program on TV. I began to have this growing desire to go to church.

We went to church occasionally growing up; however, it was far from a regular occurrence. I still had the Bible I started reading in elementary school. I remember feeling ashamed as I wiped the dust off it.

Not long after this, I went to the McDonald's across the street from campus for lunch. An upperclassman came over and started telling me that I needed to have a relationship with Jesus. It was as though I could feel the good in him, as if God were speaking through him. I confessed my sins and received Jesus as my Lord and Savior that day while sitting in McDonald's. I remember feeling so clean.

I eventually got the courage to call my mom and tell her that I was struggling and needed her to come. I finally told her about everything that happened to me. She believed everything I said, but she was in a dilemma because so many years had passed. She didn't know what to do about the family members who hurt me. I told her not to do anything. They couldn't hurt me anymore.

I started going to a counselor to talk things through, something I should have done long ago. When I changed my major to accounting, my grades started to improve. I managed to keep my scholarship. I got help dealing with my guilt and confusion. I learned a lot about how these experiences shaped my personality.

I tended to avoid confrontations when possible. I was manipulative. I didn't come right out and ask for what I wanted. I would get what I wanted by making someone think it was their idea. I started to work on these things. I became more forthcoming with people. I still tend to shy away from confrontations, though. I have to force myself to speak up at times instead of shutting down.

The greatest struggle was not just to put these things behind me but to forgive those who hurt me. Forgiveness gave me the freedom to live beyond the pain and shame.

Chapter 6

SAVED BY GRACE

During my junior year of college, I started dating a guy who went to college in a neighboring town. For the sake of privacy, I'll call him Ty. We met at the mall where he worked while I was with some of my sorority sisters. He was very handsome. There was an instant attraction. For our first date, he asked me to go to church with him. This caused me to lower my guard around him. Even though I had started going to church myself and received my salvation, I was backsliding at the time. I wasn't living my life to please God.

We'd been dating for about a month and had become intimate before the unthinkable happened. Ty stayed in an off-campus apartment with a roommate. I'll call him Cameron. While I was alone in his room one weekend, I saw a vision of the two of us being shot to death in his bed. I quickly brushed it off and told myself I was watching too much TV. I didn't know that Cameron had a shotgun, a rifle, and a crossbow in his bedroom.

Ty and Cameron did not get along, but I was always nice to him. The same night I had that vision, Cameron knocked on the door and asked me to watch some steaks that he had put in the oven while he picked up his girlfriend. I told him that I would do that for him. Ty came back from the store before Cameron returned. When he realized what I was doing, he told me to just let the steaks burn. I'm so glad that I didn't listen to him.

The following weekend, I went to visit Ty again. This time, I had my little sister with me. She slept on the couch. The weekend was uneventful. We made it back to my campus safely after our stay. The following day, I tried to call Ty. I kept getting a busy signal. I happened to be listening to the radio the following morning and heard about an off-campus shooting involving students at Ty's university. Multiple people were shot.

I later learned that Ty and Cameron had another argument. Cameron was getting high on PCP. I kept getting a busy signal because Cameron shot Ty's arm while Ty was holding the phone in the living room, trying to call the police. If Ty hadn't been a muscular person, the blast would have blown his arm off. He was also shot in both legs and his hand as he attempted to escape from the apartment. Ty had some friends visiting him at the time. One of them had two fingers blown off. Another got shrapnel in his chest as he dove behind the couch to take cover. They were all able to make it out of the apartment alive. Cameron turned the gun on himself and took his life.

Needless to say, it was a "come to Jesus" moment for many people. It seemed like everyone was getting saved! I just watched.

Until this point, I had not seen anyone who claimed to be a Christian really living the life of Christ. I backslid because I wasn't in a good church that was rightly dividing the word of God. I gravitated toward people who said they were Christians but were still drinking, partying, and having sex before marriage.

I'm not saying that you have to be perfect if you're a Christian. However, the closer you get to God, you begin to love what he loves and hate what he hates. Your desires begin to change. I was told that if I think about doing something that wasn't pleasing to God, it was the same as doing it, so I might as well just do it.

It didn't take long before I forgot about pleasing God. I didn't hear anything about casting down thoughts that were against the knowledge of God (2 Corinthians 10:5–6, KJV).

By the grace of God, Ty recovered from his injuries. If he didn't tell anyone, no one would even know that anything happened to him. We dated for about two and a half years after this incident. Having the close call didn't make me think enough about what I was doing to change.

Chapter 7

A TRUE DIVINE RELATIONSHIP

My relationship with Ty was destined to fail. The foundation of our relationship was lust. We didn't really have a lot in common. There were times when I struggled to think of things to say. The best way to start any relationship is with friendship.

After graduation, I tried to find a job in banking in the city where Ty lived. Nothing opened up for me. I still had my part-time job at McDonald's. They gave me a "big" twenty-five-cent raise to become a manager. I knew I did not want to be there when the fall semester started. It would look good on my resume, so I accepted the position anyway.

My mom told me about a job fair in a town over four and a half hours away. Out of desperation, I went to the job fair and got a job offer as a part-time payment clerk for a gas company. Where would I live? I reached out to one of my half-sisters from my dad's first marriage about the possibility of living with her. She said, "Yes!"

I put in my notice at my job. I had everything packed up and ready to go. The night before I planned to leave, I called her to work out the time I should arrive. She had changed her mind about letting me stay with her. She said that even though we were sisters, she didn't feel obligated to help me. I didn't get upset about it. We stayed on the call for a while longer, talking about other things.

That night, before I went to bed, I said a quick prayer. "Lord, if it's your will for me to make this move, prepare a place for me to stay." The next day, I had two places to choose from! I chose to stay with a girl from my hometown. We went to the same high school and college. She was older than I was, so she already had a job and an apartment of her own.

I started working about a week after I moved in with her. My job was part-time and entry-level. I was only making $120 per week. Of course, I could not survive on that. I applied for more jobs. I spent over $100 on a professional resume.

I thought it would be easy to get a job in a big city with my accounting degree, but nothing was opening up. I finally decided to apply for a cashier job at Kmart. They hired me. Now my weekly salary increased to a whopping $200, and I started to get discouraged.

Around this time, I reconnected with one of my cousins. It just so happened that she worked ten minutes from where I lived. Coincidentally, she was having car trouble and needed a ride home after work. I picked her up and drove her home. During those rides, she would start talking to me about God. She told me that nothing was going to work out for me until I got my life right with God. She invited me to visit her church. Unfortunately, what she was saying to me was going in one ear and out the other. I felt I was too young to be concerned with eternity. I wanted to live my life without being hindered by religion.

I knew her entire church schedule:

Tuesday night: praise team rehearsal
Wednesday night: Bible study
Thursday night: choir rehearsal,
Friday night: service on the 1st and 3rd Fridays
Sunday morning: service

I had no intention of becoming involved with her church activities. Then something unexpected happened. While I was processing payments for the gas company, people started sending gospel pamphlets with their bill payments. By the end of the day, I would have a stack of them. They were echoing what my cousin had been telling me.

I said to myself, *Maybe I do need to go to church.*

The first time I visited was during a Wednesday night Bible study. It was unlike the traditional Baptist or Methodist churches that I had visited in the past. There were praise dancers and several musicians. It was very lively!

I heard a beautiful voice behind me. After praise and worship ended, there was a time of fellowship. During this time, we walked around, hugging and greeting everyone. I immediately turned around to find the owner of that beautiful voice.

Once I satisfy my curiosity, I usually move on. I just had to tell her how beautiful her voice was. The usual response to such a compliment would be "Thank you."

What she said surprised and shocked me. She looked me in my eyes and said, "The devil is going to send men your way to trap you." Then she just walked away.

To say I was left speechless would be an understatement. The words she spoke to me would later draw me even closer to God.

After the service, my cousin introduced me to the pastor. He asked me if I needed a car or a place to stay. I told him that I just needed a full-time job. Everything else would fall into place once I was financially stable. He prayed with me that night. I went back to the church the following Sunday.

I made a deal with God. I said that if the choir sang a song I liked, I would go up to the altar and rededicate my life to him. I wasn't a fan of gospel music, so I was still trying to give myself a way out of this whole church thing.

Needless to say, the choir sang one of the few songs that I knew and liked—"Silver & Gold" by Kirk Franklin. I'm not sure what the pastor spoke about that day. I was just waiting for the service to end so that I could keep my end of the deal that I made with God.

A week later, I saw an ad in the paper for an accounts receivable assistant at a local television station. I felt that this would be a fun place to work. I applied for the job, and they hired me! I stayed with this company for over twenty years. I became the second person in the entire Fox Television Stations Group to start in an entry-level position and work up to the director of finance position!

I became a faithful covenant member of my church. My pastor made the Bible so easy to understand and apply to my everyday life. Seeing the musicians playing during Praise & Worship made me long to play the violin again. My mom sold the one that I had because I didn't think I would play it anymore. I didn't pick it up again after my high school graduation, so it had sat in my closet collecting dust. I regretted giving my mom permission to sell it. When I told my pastor that I used to play the violin, he bought one for me! I still play it every Sunday with the other Power of Praise Musicians.

One evening after Wednesday night Bible study, as I drove into the apartment complex, I noticed a police car. I immediately looked down to check my speedometer to make sure I wasn't speeding. It seemed like I was being watched by whoever was in that car. Confident that I hadn't broken any speeding laws, I parked my car and headed into my building.

That same police car drove up beside me, and the officer called me by name! My hand flew up to my heart. The first thought that ran through my mind was that I had been framed for something. How else would a police officer that I had never seen before know my name?

Apparently, he and some friends came through my line at the Kmart where I worked. He saw my name on my badge. I didn't remember him at all. He gave me a business card and told me to call if I ever needed anything. He was the courtesy officer for the complex where I was staying with my friend.

A few weeks later, I did need to call him. I was locked out of the apartment. My roommate hadn't gotten home yet. He was going to let me in. Before the officer came with the master key, my roommate returned, so I no longer needed his services.

When I called back to let him know that he didn't need to come over, he invited me out to dinner. I was not turning down any free meals. We were going to the Waffle House down the street. I drove myself there. It seemed harmless. He was nice.

During our meal, he asked me to go to Florida with him. He was going there for a police conference. I could see where this was heading. I knew I wasn't going to have my own room. I politely declined his offer and thanked him for dinner.

The next day, I called to thank him again. His whole demeanor changed. It wasn't what he said, but how he said it. I remembered the words that the lady said to me during my first visit to church: "The devil is going to send men your way to trap you!"

I gasped. I said to myself, "It's a trap!" and quickly hung up the phone.

My cousin called me the next day and told me to pack my bags. She wanted me to move in with her and her family. I agreed without hesitation. The timing of this was amazing because I hadn't even told her about the situation with the officer! I thought more about my first interaction with him. I wondered if he followed me from the apartment complex to work. Unless he was just really good at his job, how else would he know my car and recognize me at night without my uniform? I was so thankful that God got me out of that situation quickly.

***

As I was getting established in a new city and with my new job, I was still trying to hold on to my relationship with Ty. We tried to visit each other as much as possible. After I moved, we were four hours apart. During Ty's last visit to me, he tried to talk me into moving back with him. There was no guarantee that I would be able to find another TV station job, so I refused. It was a good thing, too. A few days later, I found out that he had gotten his ex-girlfriend pregnant. I can't remember the excuses he gave me. He did say he was stuck in the situation with his ex and the baby, but I could always turn my back and walk away.

I didn't end the relationship after hearing this news. I knew that his ex-girlfriend had never stopped trying to rekindle their relationship. I read many of the letters that she sent to him while we were together. I felt that maybe this was just another hurdle that we would have to get over. We made it through the shooting and recovery. What could be harder than that, right? I told Ty that I would pray about it and would not make a decision until God told me what to do. I decided to visit Ty and meet his son. The child was innocent, after all. While I was there, I treated the child as my own. Not long after this, I got the answer that I was seeking.

I was driving home alone after choir rehearsal at church one evening. Suddenly, I heard a voice that said, "Tomorrow night, I will give you my answer."

I started looking around in my car, even though I knew that I was alone.

The following night was the beginning of our church anniversary celebration. I was so excited! If anyone looked at me for longer than a few seconds, I wondered if God was going to use that person to speak to me. My answer finally came at the end of the service. We had a guest pastor whom I'd never met before. He gave an altar call that was unlike any that I had heard before. Usually, whoever was ministering would ask if anyone wanted to receive their salvation, wanted to join the church, or needed prayer for healing.

This pastor said, "If anyone has a problem and doesn't know what to do, come to the altar." Needless to say, I was very intrigued, though I didn't move yet. I watched the pastor go to the first person who told him her problem.

I said to myself, *You mean I need to tell him my problem? I'm not going up there.*

He went to the next person and started speaking in tongues—the Spirit's way of communicating directly with God and a manifestation of the Holy Spirit (1 Corinthians 14:2; Acts 2:4). Then he just started telling the person what to do, without any input from the person who was seeking help.

So I decided to go up to the altar.

When he got to me, the look he gave me was pity. He said, "You put your faith or trust in someone, but he let you down. You put him before God. Now it's time for you to turn your back and walk away."

I broke down and cried. I didn't know this man. I'd never seen him before in my life, yet he used the same phrase that Ty did when he told me about the baby. Ty had said that he was stuck in this situation, but I could always turn my back and walk away.

Before I got back to my seat, someone else spoke to me and said, "I believe your future husband is already here." That was also true.

God showed me that a young man from the church was meant to be my husband. Weeks earlier, two women had called me a few hours apart on a Saturday; both said the same man was interested in me. When the second woman called, I said I'd already been told the same thing that day.

She said excitedly, "In the mouth of two witnesses! In the mouth of two witnesses!"

This phrase is found in 2 Corinthians 13:1 (KJV): "In the mouth of two or three witnesses shall every word be established."

The following Sunday, we were graduating from our Sunday School courses. We were lining up in the church foyer to march into the sanctuary and receive our certificate for completing our course. The young man the two ladies mentioned to me the day before was standing in front of me. I started thinking about what they said.

I wonder... I quickly shook my head and looked away. My eyes landed on a table covered with cassette tapes containing various messages recorded by the pastor. The one that stood out was titled *In the Mouth of Two Witnesses.*

My eyes widened, and my head whipped back around to look at the man in front of me. I wanted to handle this relationship the right way. I looked through the Bible to learn how to find a husband. To my surprise, I found nothing.

I came across Proverbs 18:22 (KJV), which says, "Whoso findeth a wife findeth a good thing, and obtaineth favor of the Lord." This meant that I could not approach him. I had to wait, and wait, and wait. We were friends. It took him a year to discuss taking our relationship to the next level.

During my period of waiting, I focused on my relationship with God. I was active in the ministry. I was a violinist and also a part of the media ministry. I must say it was well worth the wait. Surprisingly, my husband was still a virgin at the age of twenty-seven.

At first, I felt unworthy, but I quickly understood that it wasn't about him. God quickly let me know that no matter what I had done or where I had been, he had already given everyone his very best—JESUS!

Before our wedding, we wrote a vision of the things we hoped to accomplish in our marriage. The title of our vision was "A True Divine Relationship." We wanted to buy a house by the time we were twenty-eight, and we were twenty-eight when we signed the contract for our first home. We planned to be married for at least three years before having children. Though our son was unexpected, he was born four days after we celebrated our third wedding anniversary.

We also dreamed of having our own business and retiring from corporate America at age thirty-five. This is the only part of our vision that has not yet come to pass. Nevertheless, a delay is not a denial.

To God be the glory, we celebrated our twenty-seventh wedding anniversary!

Chris grew up in a small southern town. His father left when he was around two years old. He believes his father left because his mom allowed her sister and her baby to move in with them to escape an abusive relationship. His father became an alcoholic. Chris was the youngest of eight children.

His mom's mother had died during childbirth. Her father remarried and moved up north, leaving her and her two younger siblings behind. She dropped out of school before graduating to help take care of her sister and brother. They moved among different relatives. She had to grow up fast.

When she had children of her own, she had to work hard to raise them alone. They didn't have much, but she was always kindhearted and willing to help anyone in need.

They lived in a big house that was very old. They had an outhouse—no indoor bathrooms. His father never supported the family after he left. That man was the father of his mom's last four children.

His best childhood memory was spending time with his mom. Just sitting around talking and sharing a meal with her was special because she was gone a lot. She always worked two or three jobs to keep food on the table and the bills paid. She would be gone from sunup to sundown. However, she did make time to train her children to be respectful to others and live decent lives.

His aunt and his older siblings took care of him when his mom was working. He was a very good baseball player, but he only remembers seeing her at one of his high school games.

When they could, they went to the tomato field to pick tomatoes. They also cleaned fish together, which wasn't one of his favorite things.

As he was growing up, he was selected as most likely to succeed and prom king. His mom always told him that he was different. He stayed out of trouble. He always wanted to look nice. She made sure he and his siblings were dressed well. His aunt's boyfriend took him under his wing. He also taught him to always be respectful, no matter what his father did or did not do. Chris didn't hold any grudges.

His mom made sure that they went to church, including Vacation Bible School. She used to clean two or three churches every weekend. Chris would go with her to help. He always wanted to have a better life. He would sit on his front porch and pray for a better future. While he was in college, he met a friend who invited him to the church where we met.

Curious, I asked him what stood out to him about me and what attracted him to me. He said I was nice and caring and that he believed I loved God. Our pastor told him that he would find a good wife because he was faithful in the ministry and always telling others about Jesus. He eventually made peace with his father. Chris took me to meet him before we got married. His father thought Chris wanted something, but he just wanted to introduce his future bride to him.

He wishes his dad had been there when he was growing up, but he's okay anyway. He survived. God has a plan for everything.

I remember when our son was born. It took three days before I even changed his diaper. I had to ask Chris to let me do it too! He was doing all the work. Chris would wake up when he heard our son's cries in the middle of the night, change him, and bring him to me so that I could feed him.

Chris attended almost every baseball game. During our son's younger years, he also helped coach his sports teams. Chris poured all the love and attention that he didn't receive from his father into our son.

Our marriage is not perfect. We go through things. We both may get on each other's nerves at times, but we never go to bed angry. After all these years, we still laugh together, chase each other around the house, take long walks, and still believe the best is yet to come. We are overcomers!

Chapter 8

SIGNS, MIRACLES, AND WONDERS

I used to think that God was a faraway being. Yet I've come to realize that he is mindful of us. "What is man, that thou art mindful of him? and the son of man, that thou visitest him?" (Psalm 8:4, KJV) God is thinking of us even when we are not thinking about him. He is concerned about what concerns us. He knows the number of hairs on our heads. "But even the very hairs of your head are all numbered. Fear not therefore: ye are of more value than many sparrows." (Luke 12:7, KJV) He is amazingly still performing miracles today!

ANOINTED TEETH

Going to the dentist has never been one of my favorite things to do. Due to my heart condition, I have to take amoxicillin an hour before my appointment to prevent any infections. During a regular cleaning, they told me I had two cavities. I was in denial, so I asked for a copy of the X-ray. I kept procrastinating about scheduling an appointment for the fillings. In the meantime, during a Sunday service, my pastor told us to place our hands on the area where we wanted God to heal. I put my hand on my mouth and asked God to remove those cavities. I still kept making excuses about going back to the dentist.

When I got pregnant with my son, I didn't want the antibiotics to affect him. After he was born, I nursed him for ten months and didn't want my breast milk to be tainted with amoxicillin. I finally went back to the dentist after four years. I should have had those two cavities and more. To my delight, I didn't have any cavities! I was so excited I almost jumped out of the chair. It's been over twenty years since then. I still haven't had any cavities. I've never had a cap, crown, filling, or root canal. My teeth are anointed!

SUPERNATURAL PROVISIONS

I did not grow up going to church regularly. Nobody ever taught me about tithing and giving offerings to God. I didn't see how I could afford to give ten percent of my gross earnings when I was struggling to pay my bills. I learned that God wants us to depend on him as little children would.

I thought back to when I was a child. I didn't worry about how bills would be paid or where my next meal would come from. I had to learn to trust God. There were times when I only had twenty dollars left for food until the next payday. I gave that last twenty as an offering.

Before I left church, someone came up to me and said, "God told me to give this to you."

It was the same amount that I gave! I never went hungry. I remember saying, "Lord, if you want me to eat, you'll feed me, but if you want me to fast, I'll fast."

The next day, my supervisor stopped in front of my desk and said, "It's been a while since I've taken everyone out to lunch. Let's all go out to lunch on me today." I could have asked my mom or stepdad for help. However, this was all building my faith.

One evening, when I was in my apartment, I said, "Lord, I need money for my rent or my car note. I can't afford to pay both." The next day was Wednesday night Bible study. Before I got to my seat, a church member stopped me. He asked, "How much is your car note? How much is your rent? I'll pay your car note."

I didn't tell anyone about this, but God touched someone's heart and moved on my behalf! Needless to say, I was amazed. When I came home that night, I was looking around my apartment to make sure it wasn't bugged. God hears us and knows our needs before we even ask. "...for your Father knoweth what things ye have need of before ye ask him." (Matthew 6:8, KJV)

When we pay tithes and give offerings, God will open the windows of heaven to bless us! "Bring ye all the tithes into the storehouse, that there may be meat in mine house, and prove me now herewith, saith the Lord of hosts, if I will not open you the windows of heaven, and pour you out a blessing, that there shall not be room enough to receive it." (Malachi 3:10, KJV)

HEPATITIS

One summer, I noticed my eyes looked strange. I had jaundice. My eyeballs were yellow instead of white. I went to the doctor, and he told me that I tested positive for hepatitis. Somehow, the part of the test that classified it as type A, B, or C got lost. I needed to go in for another test. Before my next appointment, I went to church.

During the altar call, my pastor prayed for me. He said, "Nothing is wrong with you. This is just a smoke screen."

I had the retest, and the results came back negative! I did not have hepatitis, but my eyes were still discolored. My liver enzyme levels were elevated. I was referred to a liver specialist. My prayer was that I would not be a burden to my husband or miss work. God answered my prayer. I didn't miss a day of work. I was only in pain during the wee hours of the morning. I sometimes forgot that I was sick because my husband still made me feel beautiful.

The doctor couldn't prescribe anything because the origin of my condition was unknown. I got over my fear of needles because I had to have blood drawn every week. The next step was a liver biopsy. I asked God to spare me. I did not want to go through that because I would be awake for the procedure. Before the biopsy was scheduled, my liver enzymes returned to normal levels, and my eyes were no longer yellow!

SUPERNATURAL CHILDBIRTH

About six months before I got pregnant with my son, I had a dream that I had a baby, and it didn't hurt! I was so excited that I told my husband about it right away when I woke up.

He said, "I don't know what you are dreaming about that for."

We weren't trying to have a baby at that time. I was still taking birth control pills. However, after I started seeing the liver specialist that I mentioned earlier, I had to stop taking my pills. It took a few months for my jaundice to clear up and for my liver enzymes to return to normal. During that time, my son was conceived. I was waiting for my cycle to start so that I could resume taking my birth control pills. That cycle never came. I finally decided to take a pregnancy test. Since I had been taking birth control pills for several years, I was very surprised to learn that I was pregnant after being off the pill for such a short period of time.

When I was about three months pregnant, one of my church members gave me a book titled *Supernatural Childbirth* by Jackie Mize. When I say the title, I immediately remember the dream that I had months earlier. I said, "Lord, you are really going to do this!"

> *Pregnancy and childbirth are often perceived as times of pain and hardship. In Supernatural Childbirth, Jackie Mize shares her journey to achieving a joyful, pain-free childbirth experience guided by her faith and Biblical teachings. Through personal accounts interwoven with spiritual insights, Mize provides a pathway for women to embrace pregnancy and childbirth as a miraculous, pain-free experience. She emphasizes the power of affirmations, unwavering belief, and trust in God's promises to cultivate a spiritually enriched perspective on bringing new life into the world.*
>
> ~Shortform Book Summary

Her testimony inspired me. Jackie was initially told that she would never have children. She ended up having four, two boys and two girls! Her last three pregnancies were pain-free. God treats everyone equally, regardless of background or status. I believed that if he did it for her, he could do it for me.

Before I got pregnant, my maximum weight was 107 pounds. I prayed that my baby would be at least eight pounds. That way, I would know without a shadow of a doubt that God had answered my prayer. I prayed about my son's facial features, including his complexion, while he was still in my womb. I also asked God what I should name him.

While I was driving to work one morning, I heard the name Daniel. I went into labor about 5 a.m. on a Saturday. It really wasn't a painful experience. On a scale of 1–10, it was a 1. At 8 p.m., I decided to go to the hospital because I didn't want to mess around and have my baby at home. My pregnancy triage nurse was surprised that I didn't ask for any pain medication. The nurse in the birthing room told me to let her know when

I was having a contraction because she couldn't tell by looking at me. They told me that due to my size, my baby would likely weigh no more than six and a half pounds.

The closer I got to delivery, the stronger the contractions became. When it was time to push, I felt pressure but no pain! The room was so quiet when he was born that you could hear a pin drop. The umbilical cord was wrapped around his throat.

I said, "Lord, you named him. He has to be okay."

He was passed to other people in the room while I was being cleaned up. Soon, we heard the beautiful sound of him crying. Daniel was 8 pounds and 15 ounces! "God can do exceeding abundantly above all we ask or think." (Ephesians 3:20, KJV) He looked exactly how I described him when he was still in my womb. Then God topped it off by reminding me about the vision that my husband and I wrote before we got married. We wanted to wait at least three years before having any children. Daniel was born on Mother's Day, four days after our third wedding anniversary!

OPEN HEART SURGERY

Earlier in this book, I spoke about my heart condition that was detected when I was two years old. I had regular checkups with a cardiologist every six months. They didn't seem overly concerned about anything, so I wasn't either. Then one morning when I woke up, it felt as if two fingers were nudging my heart with every beat. It wasn't painful, but it was different from anything that I had ever felt before. I called the heart clinic to see if they could fit me in for an appointment.

By the time I got there, I felt fine, but in reality, I was far from being okay. Apparently, every time my heart beat, over 50 percent of my blood was backing up into my lungs and not circulating. My first thought was, *How am I even functioning?* The answer to that was simple: it was the grace of God!

I was referred to a heart surgeon the same day. Two months later, I had open-heart surgery. There were complications after the surgery. My heart's natural electrical pathways never came back into sync. Now I am pacemaker dependent. You might wonder where the blessing is in this. Well, because I didn't ignore the symptoms, I'm still alive.

After surgery, I was on about seven different medications. I was weaned off all of them within ninety days. I had that surgery over ten years ago. I'm still not on any prescription drugs. I take an Aspirin a day and some heart health vitamins that my pastor told me about. I learned that it was unheard of, given the type of surgery I had. God is so *good*!

Chapter 9

TURNING SCARS INTO STARS

Some people spend their entire lives reacting to the bad things that have happened to them. I was one of those people who suffered in silence for years. We put on a mask and hide from the world. We bury our traumas so that we don't have to face them. Don't let what happened to you control the rest of your life. You can't fix what you don't face. God can't heal what you won't reveal. An untreated wound can lead to serious complications like infections, tissue death, and even sepsis, potentially requiring amputation in serious cases. Hidden pain can also cause serious damage.

I want you to come to Jesus. "We overcome by the blood of the Lamb, and by the word of our testimony!" (Revelation 12:11, KJV)

Read this prayer aloud.

Heavenly Father, thank You for Your great love for me.
I believe that Jesus Christ is Your Son, that he died on the Cross for me,
and that You raised him from the dead.
Please wash me clean with His blood.
Thank you for forgiving me and making me Your child.
Jesus, please come into my life right now, live in my heart, and fill me
with Your Holy Spirit.
Be my Savior and Lord.

Set me free now from every bondage the devil has held in my life.
Jesus, I pray this prayer in Your powerful name.
Amen.

If you prayed this prayer, then welcome to the family of God! According to Luke 15:10, right now the angels in heaven are rejoicing over you! (Prayer taken from *Ancient Secrets of the Tabernacle Revealed: Your Pathway to God's Presence* by David Cerullo.)

The lyrics to the song "Clean" by Natalie Grant describe what just happened to you.

Washed in the blood of Your sacrifice
Your blood flowed red and made me white
My dirty rags are purified
I am clean, I am clean...

All your sins have been forgiven, past, present, and future! The next thing that you have to do is forgive the people who have hurt you. Holding on to the pain and hurt is only hurting you. Ask God to help you let it go. God did it for me. I know that he'll do the same for you! Coincidentally, as I was working on this book, I saw my uncle, whom I wrote about in Chapter 5. I was very surprised to see him because I wasn't expecting it. I haven't seen him in over twenty years. However, I remained calm. I realized that I had forgiven him. He no longer had any power over me. I was able to speak cordially to him. When I walked away, my thoughts didn't linger on him or what he did to me.

"If the Son therefore shall make you free, ye shall be free indeed." (John 8:36 KJV)

"...forgetting those things which are behind, and reaching forth unto those things which are before." (Philippians 3:13, KJV)

You can't move forward until you let go of your past. What happened to you does not define you. God can turn your heartache and adversity into miracle living. He has a plan for your life until your last breath. "For I know the thoughts that I think toward you, saith the LORD, thoughts of peace, and not of evil, to give you an expected end." (Jeremiah 29:11, KJV)

Don't isolate yourself. Don't feel sorry for yourself. God wants to give you double for your shame. He can turn your shame into glory! "Behold, at that time I will undo all that afflict thee: and I will save her that halteth, and gather her that was driven out; and I will get them praise and fame in every land where they have been put to shame." (Zephaniah 3:19, KJV)

"For your shame ye shall have double; and for confusion they shall rejoice in their portion: therefore, in their land they shall possess the double: everlasting joy shall be unto them." (Isaiah 61:7, KJV)

My pastor has allowed me to share some passages from his books that I believe will help you in your journey. These excerpts come from *The Journey of the Blood* by Apostle H.L. Horton & Apostle Frank Baio (pages 51–91).

When Jesus was crucified, he shed his blood in seven places.

1. In the Garden of Gethsemane, Jesus won back our willpower that Adam lost in the Garden of Eden. Jesus said, "Not my will, Lord, but thy will be done."

2. The stripes on Jesus' back won back our health. He was flogged 39 times for all diseases. There are 39 root diseases in the world. Each stripe was for the sake of every sickness man would ever suffer from.

3. Jesus' crown of thorns won back our prosperity. This redeemed us from the curse of poverty.

4. Jesus' pierced hands won back dominion over the things we touch. Everything we put our hands to God will cause us to prosper because of this.
5. Jesus' pierced feet won back dominion over the places we walk. This blood redeemed us from our loss of dominion and authority.
6. Jesus' pierced heart won back our joy when the soldier shoved a spear into his side to be sure he was dead.
7. Jesus' bruises won our deliverance from inner hurts and iniquities.

If you have a deep bruise inside, perhaps from divorce, suicidal tendencies, or sexual abuse, Jesus bore your hurts and bruises so that you can be whole again.

God sent Jesus to heal the broken-hearted. The enemy may have done many things to crush your heart and will to live. You may have gone through many things at the hands of men, but when we come to Jesus, broken hearts are made new again. Regardless of what has been done against you by anyone to break your heart, the heart of Jesus was broken so that yours can be made whole again. You can have a brand-new heart from the Master today! You can have your joy restored. No more sad and gloomy depressed days, for joy has been repurchased for you!

"He healeth the broken in heart, and bindeth up their wounds." (Psalm 147:3, KJV)

When Jesus died on the Cross, he covered our past, present, and future sins. You are not an old sinner saved by grace. This type of thinking keeps you sin-conscious. He who is dead is free from sin. Your old man has been killed off. Religion would have you think that you escaped death. Nowhere in the Bible does it record that you escaped death. "For ye are dead and your life is hid in Christ in God." (Colossians 3:3, KJV)

What God does is forever. The devil can't take your salvation. Whatever God does, no one can take it away from you. This is why Romans 8:35 (KJV) says, "Who shall separate us from the love of God? Shall tribulation, or distress, or persecution, or famine, or nakedness, or peril, or sword?" Nothing and no one can pluck you out of the Father's hand. Some sins in your life might come up, but the blood of Jesus will cover your imperfect soul and corrupt body. Thank God for the blood of Jesus. It will never lose its power! You have an incorruptible seed inside of you if you prayed with me at the beginning of this chapter. "Being born again, not of corruptible seed, but of incorruptible, by the word of God, which liveth and abideth for ever." (1 Peter 1:23, KJV) Whatever God does, it shall be forever. You can rest assured of that.

No sin and no events are beyond his power to touch and redeem. When Jesus died on the Cross, he covered everything. He covered your growing up, getting old, divorces, and fornication. The Cross was a legal transaction. God does everything legally.

That's why the Bible says in Romans 8:33 (KJV), "Who shall lay anything to the charge of God's elect." You can't be charged because whatsoever God does is forever. God loves you all the way through eternity!

When you were born again, God perfected your spirit. What God is working on now is your soul—how you think, want, and feel—and teaching you how to keep your body under subjection. This is a lifetime process. That is what the blood of Jesus is for.

Pray for God to lead you to a good church, one that teaches the whole Bible

from Genesis to Revelation. Pray for a pastor like the one described in Jeremiah 3:15 (KJV): "And I will give you pastors according to mine heart, which shall feed you with knowledge and understanding."

As you go to church, you get the seed watered. The seed is the word of God. The more of the word of God you get in you, the stronger you will become, and you will know who you are in Christ.

As a born-again believer, you are a part of the Body of Christ. When we go to church, God is assembling His body. The Bible says that we are "fitly joined together" (Ephesians 4:16, KJV). Our individual roles and functions are vital to the body's overall well-being.

Here's a practical example. Would you consider walking out of your house and leaving your foot, hand, or brain behind? The answer is "No!" You need all of your body parts together to function at your peak! The same is true of the body of Christ. Every member of the body is important.

The following are excerpts from *The Apostle's Nuggets: Poured Out Revelations With Sips of Insight* by Apostle H. L. Horton.

According to the word of God, you are:

1. New creation
2. Heir of God
3. Joint-heir with Jesus
4. In perfect health
5. Blessed with every spiritual blessing
6. Free from want
7. In favor with God and man
8. Saved
9. Redeemed
10. More than a conqueror
11. Abiding in him
12. Set apart
13. Forgiving
14. Partaker of his Divine nature

15. Delivered from evil
16. Blessed of the Father
17. Strong in him and the power of his might
18. Walking in victory
19. A member of the royal family
20. Reigning in life

There are more, but I only listed twenty because twenty in the Bible is the number of expectation. Expect God to do great things in your life! Don't let your pain be your prison. Don't let your pain ruin relationships, negatively impact your health, and destroy the future that God intended for you. Take this leap of faith with me. God can turn your heartache and adversities into miraculous living. He can turn your scars into stars. Let Jesus into your heart and let him lead and guide you in your journey. I promise you won't recognize your life. You can love and be loved. You can be free!

Chapter 10

SUPERNATURAL ASSISTANCE FOR A SUPERNATURAL EXISTENCE

You can find the following prayers in *The Apostle's Nuggets: Poured Out Revelations with Sips of Insight* by Apostle H. L. Horton.

FAITH CONFESSIONS THAT SWALLOW THE ENEMY (PAGE 72)

Lord, you are the God who swallows your enemies. You swallowed Pharoah in the Red Sea (Exodus 14:28). You swallowed Korah in the earth because of his rebellion (Numbers 16:32). You caused the earth to swallow the flood released by the dragon (Rev 12:16). You prepared a great fish to swallow up Jonah (Jonah 1:17). Let all poverty and lack be swallowed up in the name of Jesus. Let all sickness and diseases be swallowed up in the name of Jesus. Let all discouragement and defeat be swallowed up in the name of Jesus. Let all assignments of hell against my life be swallowed up in the name of Jesus. In the name of Jesus, let all generational curses and negative words spoken against my life be swallowed up in the name of Jesus. Let all of the rods of the enemy be swallowed up in the name of Jesus. Let all hurts and wounds in my childhood be swallowed up in the name of Jesus. Fear, be swallowed up. Witchcraft, be swallowed up. Anxiety, be swallowed up. Frustration, be swallowed up. Everything that would attempt to swallow me be swallowed up in the **MIGHTY NAME OF JESUS!!!**

LEAP CONFESSIONS FOR SUDDEN INCREASE AND SUPERNATURAL ASSISTANCE (PAGE 44)

"I can run through a troop and leap over a wall." (Psalm 18:29, KJV)

Let my steps turn into leaps, in the name of Jesus.

I leap past all distractions in the name of Jesus.

I leap over every wall constructed by the enemy.

In the name of Jesus, I leap ahead of satanic strategies that have illegally jumped ahead of me.

I will leap over my enemies like David.

In the name of Jesus, with excitement, I leap into my future.

In the name of Jesus, I leap from lack to abundance.

In the name of Jesus, I leap from failure to victory.

In the name of Jesus, I take a leap of faith and do the impossible.

In the name of Jesus, let my finances grow by leaps and bounds.

In the name of Jesus, I leap to a level I have not seen before.

Let provisions and resources leap onto my life, in the name of Jesus.

Let wisdom and understanding increase by leaps and bounds in the name of Jesus.

Let favor increase in my life by leaps and bounds.

I will leap and rejoice at the goodness of God.

The Lord has given me leaping for sadness and joy for mourning.

I will leap above problems and setbacks in the name of Jesus.

I lay aside every weight and burden that will prevent me from leaping.

Let my praise and worship leap to another level.

Let my prayer life leap forward.

I will leap forward in my giving.

Let my love and faith take a quantum leap.

Let Kingdomized thinking advance in my church by leaps and bounds.

I'm sure you have noticed that "In Jesus' name" was mentioned several times in this prayer. When we pray in his name, we are coming to God with his authority and acknowledging Jesus as our mediator. "And whatsoever ye shall ask in my name, that will I do, that the Father may be glorified in the Son. If ye shall ask any thing in my name, I will do it." (John 14:13–14, KJV) "For there is one God, and one mediator between God and men, the man Christ Jesus." (1 Timothy 2:5 KJV)

God Wants to be Involved in Your Finances & You're More Than Conquering Life (Pages 39–40)

My Personal Declaration of Faith

- I am filled with the knowledge of God's will, in all wisdom and spiritual understanding. His will is my prosperity. (Colossians 1:9)
- I honor the Lord with my substance and the first fruit of my increase. My purses and wallets are filled with plenty, and my endeavors burst forth with new benefits. (Prov. 3:9–10)
- The Lord rebukes the devourer for my sake, and no weapon formed against my finances and provisions will prosper. All

obstacles and hindrances to my finances and provisions are now dissipating and vanishing. (Malachi 3:10–11; Isaiah 54:17)

- I am delivered from the power and authority of darkness. I cast down reasoning and imaginations that exalt themselves above and against the knowledge of God. I bring every idle thought into captivity into the obedience of God's word. (2 Corinthians 1:3–5; 2 Corinthians 10:5)
- The Lord causes my thoughts to become agreeable to His will, and my plans (which are his plans) are established and work for my good. (Proverbs 16:3)
- The Lord has pleasure in the prosperity of his servant because we are participating in his righteous cause. (Psalm 35:27)
- I speak life only to the end result of what I desire. I will not speak contrary to the word of God. (I will watch my words—speaking life only.)
- The Lord is my Shepherd, and I know not lack, having received the abundance of grace and the gift of righteousness. I reign as a King in life by Jesus Christ NOW!!! (Romans 5:17)

AUTHOR BIO

Tajuana Brown

Tajuana Brown has spent nearly thirty years working as an accountant for Fox Television Stations. Starting as an entry-level accounts receivable assistant and part-time switchboard operator, she climbed the corporate ladder to become the Director of Finance. Later in her career at Fox, she worked as a production accountant for various shows. She is also a violinist who plays at her local church.

Now, she steps into the literary world with her debut book, *Don't Let Your Pain Be Your Prison*, a powerful reflection on overcoming adversity, the journey of forgiveness, and the unshakable strength of faith. With heartfelt honesty and a desire to inspire others, Tajuana shares her story to encourage readers to find hope and the strength to overcome the pain of their past.

BOOKS CITED

Cerullo, David. *Ancient Secrets of the Tabernacle Revealed: Your Pathway to God's Presence.*

Horton, Halton, and Frank Baio. *The Journey of the Blood.*

Horton, Halton. *The Apostle's Nuggets.*

www.ingramcontent.com/pod-product-compliance
Lightning Source LLC
LaVergne TN
LVHW052258100826
845147LV00001B/78
* 9 7 8 1 9 6 5 3 1 9 9 1 8 *